AR. 6.2
Pts. 3.0

DATE DUE

OCT 0 6 2009		

DEMCO 38-296

D1472470

Girl in the Mirror

Understanding Physical Changes

Girl in the Mirror

Understanding Physical Changes

by Ashley Rae Harris

Content Consultant
Vicki F. Panaccione, PhD
Licensed Child Psychologist
Founder, Better Parenting Institute

Credits

Published by ABDO Publishing Company, 8000 West 78th Street, Edina, Minnesota 55439. Copyright © 2009 by Abdo Consulting Group, Inc. International copyrights reserved in all countries. No part of this book may be reproduced in any form without written permission from the publisher. The Essential Library™ is a trademark and logo of ABDO Publishing Company.

Printed in the United States.

Special thanks to Dr. Vicki Panaccione for her expertise and guidance in shaping this series.

Editors: Jill Sherman, Patricia Stockland
Copy Editor: Erika Wittekind
Interior Design and Production: Becky Daum
Cover Design: Becky Daum

Library of Congress Cataloging-in-Publication Data
Harris, Ashley Rae.
  Girl in the mirror : understanding physical changes / by Ashley Rae Harris.
    p. cm. — (Essential health: strong, beautiful girls)
  Includes index.
  ISBN 978-1-60453-100-8
  1. Body image in adolescence—Juvenile literature. I. Title.

BF724.3.B55H37 2009
155.5'33—dc22
                        2008011903

Contents

Meet Dr. Vicki

Throughout the series Strong, Beautiful Girls, you'll hear the reassuring, knowledgeable voice of Dr. Vicki Panaccione, a licensed psychologist with more than 25 years of experience working with teens, children, and families. Dr. Vicki offers her expert advice to girls who find themselves in the difficult situations described in each chapter.

Better known as the Parenting Professor™, Dr. Vicki is founder of the Better Parenting Institute™ and author of *Discover Your Child* and *What Your Kids Would Tell You . . . If Only You'd Ask!* You might have seen her name quoted in publications such as the *New York Times*, *Family Circle*, and *Parents* magazine.

While her credentials run deep, perhaps what qualifies her most to advise girls on everything from body image to friendship to schoolwork is that she's been there, so she can relate. "I started out in junior high as the chubby new kid with glasses and freckles, who the popular kids loved to tease or even worse . . . ignore," says the doc. "They should see me now!"

Today, Dr. Vicki maintains a private practice in Melbourne, Florida, and writes articles for a variety of periodicals and Web sites. She has been interviewed or quoted in major publications including *Parenting* magazine, *Reader's Digest*, *First for Women*, and *Woman's World*, networks such as Fox, ABC, NBC, and CBS, and several popular Web sites. Dr. Vicki joined esteemed colleagues Tony Robbins, Dr. Wayne Dyer, and Bill Bartmann as coauthor of *The Power of Team*, the latest in the best-selling series Wake Up and Live the Life You Love. She is an adviser for the Web site parentalwisdom.com and also for MTV/Nickelodeon's parentsconnect.com. She is a clinical consultant for Red Line Editorial, Inc. Not to mention, she's the proud mother of Alex, her 21-year-old son who is pursuing his PhD to become a medical researcher.

With all that she has going for her now, it might be hard to imagine that Dr. Vicki was ever an awkward teen struggling to find her way. But consider this—she's living proof that no matter how bleak things might look now, they do get better. The following stories and Dr. Vicki's guidance will help you discover your own path to happiness and success, becoming the Strong, Beautiful Girl you are meant to be.

Take It from Me

When I was asked to write a book about self-esteem for middle-school girls, I thought immediately about my own adolescence. I was a chubby preteen with braces. Even though I wasn't lazy and I didn't eat any more junk food than my friends did, the extra weight seemed to stick to me more than it did to them. My chubby tummy never looked right in the trendy clothes I wanted to wear, and I skipped swimming in gym so I wouldn't have to wear a bathing suit.

I wished then that I could read something that really captured how I felt, which was as if my outside didn't match my inside. I felt as though I'd been dealt a bad hand and would have to work harder than everyone else just to prove that I was fun, stylish, and worthy of friends and attention from boys.

Since talking to many girls and women about this book, I realize now that I was not alone in my insecurities about my body. Fat girls, little girls, and early developers all struggle with their body images. Most of us do not want to stick out in the crowd, but sometimes it can't be helped, such as when you're the only person of your race in school or if you have a disability.

Even the things that we can change about ourselves make some girls insecure. "Tomboys" and "lame dressers" may not know how to make the adjustment to middle-school style.

This book can't talk about every annoying feature we obsess about when gazing in the mirror. But I hope that by reading it you'll start to realize that you're not alone in your concerns about body image—and even start thinking about your own body in a different, happier way.

XOXO,
Ashley

1

The Fat Girl

Of the many awkward labels a young girl can face, probably few are as painful as being pegged the "fat girl." When you're the "fat kid," being made fun of is part of the daily routine. It's as common as making fun of the teacher or complaining about the homework. The fact of the matter is that being overweight is really hard. Kids who struggle with their weight may have fewer friends, more difficulty with schoolwork than their peers, or even develop eating disorders.

Most preteens are awkward in more ways than one. Certain body parts grow faster than others. Hair starts to appear unexpectedly in places it never was before. Skin may become greasy or pimply. But kids who are overweight have another mark against them: other people assume that it is their fault. And if you're the "fat kid," it can be easy to believe them. You may even blame yourself for being that way. You might think that you're not a good person or that there's something wrong with you.

Worse, girls who are overweight have another problem to face. Almost every woman or girl who is considered to be beautiful in magazines, movies, at school, or even at home, is skinny—or at least on the thin side. You might have great hair and a pretty smile, but if you're overweight, chances are you don't even think that there is a chance you could be pretty.

But, we shouldn't forget another part of the picture. Even though skinny girls are everywhere on television, more and more real girls are struggling with their weight. Maybe it has to do with eating more fast food or spending more time inside watching television. The point is, more girls than ever before have to deal with the hurt and shame that go along with carrying some extra pounds.

> **More girls than ever before have to deal with the hurt and shame that go along with carrying some extra pounds.**

Lindsey's Story

Lindsey was a quiet girl. She usually listened to her iPod on the bus to school and kept to herself once she

got there. Her teachers said she was shy and didn't mix well with the other kids. The truth was, Lindsey was overweight.

   She wore adult-woman jeans in the fifth grade. Her baggy sweaters covered most of her body, and when she walked down the hallway, other kids would call her "the Blob." Sometimes she heard them say it, but she marched past them with a blank stare, pretending she didn't hear them. But she really did . . . and it really hurt.

Lindsey always had been on the chubby side and was used to being teased about her weight both at school and at home. Her dad said things like, "If you keep eating all that chocolate, you'll end up fat just like your mother." It was true that Lindsey's mom was overweight too, and she hated when people compared them to one another.

Talk About It

- **How do you think Lindsey feels?**
- **Have you ever been teased about your weight? How did it feel? What did you do?**
- **Have you ever pretended that what other people said about you didn't matter, even when it really did?**

Lindsey longed to be thin. She spent many hours flipping through teen magazines filled with skinny models. She even tried to diet with her mom and do sit-ups and push-ups in her room. She was too embarrassed about her size to exercise outside, where someone might see her.

One month, Lindsey tried especially hard to eat less and exercise in her bedroom every night. She was very hungry, and her stomach would grumble after skipping lunch, but she kept on, wishing it would make her thin.

One day, she thought she might have lost a little weight, so she tried on a pair of jeans that had become too tight to zip all the way. To her surprise, she was able to zip them up!

Talk About It

- Have you ever tried different ways to lose weight? Did they work?
- What do you think about Lindsey's way of trying to lose weight? Can you come up with other solutions?

Feeling proud of herself, Lindsey wore the jeans to school the next day. Still in a good mood during math class, she volunteered to do a problem on the board. But as she walked up to the front of the room, she heard a boy from the back row say, "Look at how tight Fat Lindsey's pants are!" He laughed with his friends.

Lindsey's face turned bright red. Normally she could ignore mean comments, but not today, when she'd been feeling good about herself.

When she came home from school, Lindsey turned on the television. She felt like no matter what she did, she would always be fat. Then, she went into the kitchen and found a box of her mother's favorite cookies. She ate one, then another. She kept eating them until the box was empty, all the while thinking about how no one would ever see her as anything but fat.

> **Lindsey felt like no matter what she did, she would always be fat.**

Talk About It

- **Why did Lindsey feel more embarrassed when she was teased on the day she wore the jeans than all the other days at school?**

- **Have you ever had a really embarrassing moment at school? How did you handle it?**

- **Why do you think Lindsey ate the cookies? How could Lindsey have reacted differently to the situation?**

- **Have you ever used food for comfort when upset? Did it help? How did you feel?**

Oftentimes, when people are overweight, they feel guilty and ashamed of themselves. They start to think that they don't deserve the same things that other people deserve. In a way, the bigger their bodies become, the smaller their personalities become inside.

Lindsey hasn't even had a chance to figure out what kind of person she is or what she wants to do with her life. Yet, she is already beginning to think that she isn't worth anything. And, she is putting all her attention on her weight, rather than looking at her positive qualities.

Often, embarrassment and guilt keep girls from reaching out for help. It is important for girls who are struggling with their weight to find a trusted adult to talk to about what's going on. If they keep their feelings inside, chances are they will resort to unhealthy ways of dealing with it, such as getting comfort from food rather than from people who care.

It also is very important to remember that our looks are only one small part of who we really are. You've heard the old saying, "You can't judge a book by its cover." Well, if we judged everyone by how he or she looked, we'd be missing out on lots of opportunities to meet some really terrific people.

Get Healthy

1. Instead of skipping meals, try making a recipe from a healthy cookbook. It will taste good and give you energy. Try not to think of it as dieting, but instead think of it as a new way of eating.

2. Make exercise more fun by riding a bike or walking a dog. It's a great way to relax and breathe some fresh air.

3. Ask your mom or dad to buy you something in your size that you really want to wear, no matter how it looks on you. Even if you don't have the nerve to wear it to school, you still can wear it when you dance around your bedroom!

The Last Word from Ashley

It is better to get a grip on weight issues early. That means learning healthy ways of eating and exercising. It also means learning how to deal with your feelings in ways other than eating. Put more energy and focus into aspects of yourself that don't have to do with your weight, such as your interests and talents. You may find that you aren't doing as many unhealthy activities. Maybe the weight will even start to drop on its own. But even if it doesn't, it is important to remember that you are an important, worthy person, no matter how much you weigh.

2

The Bite Counter

Have you ever been on a diet? If you said yes, you are far from alone. Most girls have gone on multiple diets by the time they become young women. One diet might be low calorie, another low fat, and another low carbs. Some girls just cut back on what they eat, no matter what it is. Some will even go a day or more without eating anything at all.

While being overweight does have health risks, it is important to realize that not getting the right nutrition is dangerous, too. If you starve your body of the things it needs to grow and develop, not only will you not feel very well, but you may have some serious physical and emotional problems that you had not even considered before.

Have you ever known someone who either doesn't eat almost anything at all—or who eats quite a bit but then sneaks off to throw up? Those are signs of eating disorders called anorexia and bulimia. Anorexics and bulimics can suffer many side effects and health problems, such as thinning or corroding bones, hair loss, inability to sleep or sit still, arthritis, kidney and liver failure, internal bleeding, easy bruising, and rotting teeth. They may grow an extra layer of hair on their bodies and have a greater risk for heart attacks and seizures. They also can become infertile. Who knew that not eating could actually be life-threatening? Camille is about to find out.

Who knew that not eating could actually be life-threatening?

Camille's Story

Camille had heard rumors about girls in her school who had anorexia or bulimia. She wasn't worried about them, however. She had her eating under total control. She knew exactly how many bites she ate every day and the amount of calories in each and every bite. So far, her diet had been great, too. She had lost more than 20 pounds in two months, and boys that hadn't even

glanced her way before were paying attention. Even her girlfriends were noticing, although they seemed more jealous than impressed.

She thought back to the conversation she had accidentally overheard about two months ago. Tim, the boy she had had a crush on since the beginning of the school year, was talking about the upcoming Spring Fling.

"Are you going?" asked Matthew.

Tim grinned. "Yea, I think so."

"Who are you takin'?"

"I was thinking about taking Camille, actually," replied Tim. Camille's breath caught in her chest and she could feel all the blood rush to her head.

"Camille? You mean the chubby girl in our math class?" asked Matthew. "I guess she's cute—but she'd look a lot better if there was less of her."

Tim laughed and the two boys had walked off, leaving Camille in silent tears.

Talk About It

- Overhearing others talking about you can be upsetting. Has it ever happened to you? How did you feel about what you heard?

- How did this conversation change Camille's behavior?

- Have you ever tried to lose weight? What method did you select? How did it work out for you?

Camille stood looking at herself in the mirror as she remembered the sound of Tim laughing about her. She looked better—but not good enough. That would take longer. She still had fat parts on her, although at least now she could see her ribs.

"Time for dinner, Camille!" yelled Cameron, her younger brother. Camille sighed. Another meal to get through. Another game to play with her parents as she worked to hide her food and give most of it to the dog. She grabbed a sweater as she headed to the kitchen.

"I made your favorite dish, hon," said Camille's mom. "Lasagna!"

Camille winced. This was going to be harder than she had thought. She loved lasagna, but it had way too many calories to eat more than one bite. What would she do with the rest?

Talk About It

- Have you ever tried to hide food so other people wouldn't realize you were not eating it? Why did you do it?

- What advice would you like to give Camille?

- What do you see when you look in the mirror? Do you like what you see? Do you recognize the best parts about you?

Dinner had taken forever to get through, but finally Camille was able to leave the table. She had managed to only eat six bites, but that was five bites more than she should have had. She knew what that meant, and yet, it was hard to face it. She had hated throwing up since she was a little kid. She had become quite good at it, though, because she did it so often. Whenever she gave in to her cravings or ate too much like she had tonight, she made herself throw up. She knew how to do it so no one would notice. She always used the upstairs bathroom and she sucked on sugar-free mints afterward.

After cleaning up after herself in the bathroom, Camille went back into her bedroom and crawled under the covers. She seemed to feel cold all the time lately. She was quite tired but could not even think about sleeping yet. But, she knew what she could do to warm up, pass the time, and burn off some calories.

Whenever Camille gave in to her cravings or ate too much, she made herself throw up. She knew how to do it so no one would notice.

Hopping out of bed, Camille grabbed the jump rope from inside her clothes closet. She began jumping, trying to find a steady rhythm. Instead of relaxing into a pattern like usual, however, Camille began to stumble. Several times she caught her foot on the rope.

Finally she stopped for a moment. When she did, she was shocked at how fast her heart was beating. It felt like her whole body was shaking and that each beat of her heart was loud enough for the whole house to hear. It was a little scary. In fact, it was a lot scary.

Talk About It

- Why does Camille feel like she has to throw up? What effects might this have on her body?

- Why does Camille decide to exercise? Why is she so frightened a few minutes later?

- If you were with Camille right now, what would you suggest she do next?

The next day at school, Camille made a special point of hanging out around Tim. The Spring Fling dance was this weekend and as far as she could tell, he had not asked anyone to it yet. She had worn her tightest skirt that day because it showed off her flat stomach.

During lunch, Camille ran off to her locker to get the book report she had written for history class that afternoon. Just as she was about to turn the corner into the next hallway, she heard Tim's voice. He was talking to Matthew again.

"It's this weekend, Tim," stated Matthew. "Are you going to ask Camille or not?"

Tim paused, and once again Camille found that she was holding her breath.

"I don't think so," Tim finally said. "I was going to, but have you seen her lately? She is scrawny, man.

All skin and bones. I think something might be wrong with her. I'm asking Kimberly instead."

Again, tears rolled down Camille's face. She didn't get it. Would she ever look just right? What did people expect of her?

Talk About It

- **How is Camille feeling about herself?**

- **Have you ever felt like no matter what you did, you didn't fit others' expectations? What did you do about it?**

- **How do you decide what is the best way for you to look? What do you base it on?**

You truly can lose everything by devoting yourself to being thin. Eating disorders make you physically weak and ill, cold, and dizzy because without enough nutrients, your body suffers from malnutrition. You may lose interest in activities you used to enjoy. Relationships and friendships can become impossible to maintain if you are completely focused on what you are—or are not—eating.

Eating disorders, once begun, can get even more complicated as each symptom makes another worse. For example, if you force yourself not to eat, you may find that you are also physically unable to eat even if you try. If you were once bubbly and friendly, you may become quiet and withdrawn because your energy has been sucked dry from constantly starving or repeatedly vomiting.

You might find that you use food and diet as a way to deal with some of your emotions. Whether you eat too much or too little, you may be acting out how you feel inside by what you put in your mouth.

Get Healthy

1. Talk to your parents. Together, come up with some healthy options, such as cutting down on junk food in the house, cooking healthier

meals, and learning to make nutritious snacks.

2. If you find yourself skipping meals and/or making yourself throw up, talk about it with a person you trust. See what kind of ideas, assistance, and comfort he or she can give you.

3. Look in the mirror and find something about yourself that you really like. Focus on what you like best so that you face the day with a confident attitude.

4. Do not base what you should look like on any model or celebrity. Those women have been made up to look beautiful in a way that is not humanly possible.

The Last Word from Ashley

While being thin can be healthy, being too thin can be deadly. Eating disorders not only interfere with your growth but can lead to physical problems such as the loss of regular periods, heart malfunctions, and bone weakness.

If you want to lose weight, find healthy ways to do it. Eat healthy foods and eat regularly. Include a reasonable amount of exercise in your program. If weight comes off very quickly, it most likely is not coming off safely. Talk to your parents, a family doctor, or a health teacher to get some safe ideas.

3

The Little Girl

So we know being overweight is tough. I don't think anyone envied Lindsey's position or Camille's solution. But, what about girls who deal with the opposite problem, being unusually skinny and underdeveloped? "Little girls," who remain short, flat-chested, and very thin after other girls have started to grow breasts and hips, are often insecure about their lack of development.

These girls may have difficulty getting people to take them seriously. Adults talk to them as if they are much younger and don't understand what other girls their age know. They are rarely noticed for their athletic abilities. Because they look younger, parents and other authority figures may give them rules that should really be used for much younger kids.

Anyone would be jealous of my friend Milana. She is tiny and has a beautiful face and lush, blond hair that is perfectly wavy. When she first told me that she was skinny and small in middle school, I didn't feel very sorry for her. I was, after all, overweight and would have given anything to be little. But when she explained her experience, I understood just how difficult that time in her life was. Now, at age 28, she says, "It sucked." Just ask Sarah, who knows exactly how Milana felt.

Sarah's Story

Sarah was the youngest in a family of three kids. Her sister, Emily, was 14 and had tons of friends and boyfriends. Sarah was only two years younger than Emily, but she looked like she could have been four years younger. Emily looked sophisticated with lots of eye makeup and low-cut tops

Sarah looked like a little girl playing dress up whenever she tried to wear lip gloss.

that showed off her big breasts, while Sarah looked like a little girl playing dress up whenever she even tried to wear lip gloss.

Sarah had always been small for her age. It had never seemed like too big a deal—until she got to seventh grade. Now that other girls were beginning to become curvy and look older, Sarah noticed just how much younger she looked in comparison. At four feet eight inches (1.4 m), and 60 pounds (27.2 kg), with no breasts or hips, Sarah could pass for a fifth grader.

Sarah's best friend, Kammie, was way more developed. They would talk every night on the phone. They told each other everything from family secrets to which boys they had crushes on. Sarah often told Kammie how lucky she was to have hips and boobs. Kammie thought Sarah was lucky to be so skinny.

But recently, Kammie had begun to hang out with the new girl, Lauren, who had long, dark hair that she wore piled high on her head with a thick headband. Lauren was cool and came from the city, so she knew a lot about other places.

Now that Kammie was hanging out with Lauren, she had taken to styling her hair the same way and wearing more fitted clothes. Sarah noticed how much older Kammie looked and felt like a ridiculous little kid in her own baggy sweatshirt. Sarah tried on low-cut tops and tight pants, but she still looked like a little kid. Gradually, Sarah and Kammie didn't talk or hang out as much as they used to.

Talk About It

- **Why does Sarah feel like a little kid next to Kammie?**

- **Have you ever had a close friend dump you for someone "cooler"? How did it feel? What did you do?**

- **What advice would you give Sarah?**

At home, things weren't much better. At the dinner table, Sarah's parents and Emily were talking about which boys would be going to a movie that evening

Sarah could feel her face go hot and her throat get tight.

with Emily and her friends. Sarah asked to stay up to watch her favorite actor on a late-night show. Her father said, "No, Sarah, I think you are too young to stay up that late. Better get some sleep on a school night."

"But Emily got to stay up to watch TV when she was my age!" Sarah could feel her face go hot and her throat get tight. She was so mad that tears began to form.

"Sarah, don't be such a crybaby," said Emily, laughing. "It's only TV."

"Shut up, Emily!" Sarah screamed. "You get everything you want, and I have nothing. I hate everyone!"

Talk About It

- Why did Sarah get so upset? Is she upset about not being allowed to watch the TV program, or is it something more?

- How could Sarah have handled the situation differently?

"Sarah, that is quite enough," said her father. "I think it's time for you to go to your room."

Still furious, Sarah stormed up to her bedroom. She threw herself down on her bed. She was so mad that her heart was pounding in her chest.

Alone in her bedroom, Sarah thought about what had just happened. She tried to figure out why her parents treated her and her sister so differently. She regretted screaming at Emily. She realized that by losing her cool, she just proved herself to be the baby that everyone thought she was. She was so sick of being treated like a little kid. She thought that if only she were taller, with some slight curves, things would be different.

Talk About It

- **What could Sarah do to help her parents understand that she isn't a little girl anymore?**

- **What could she do to get along better with other girls her age?**

- **Have you ever felt like your parents treated you unfairly, as if you were a little kid? What would you do if you were in Sarah's position?**

Sarah probably handled the situation like a lot of people would. By the time her dad rejected her request to stay up late, she was already feeling resentful about being treated like a kid. It is difficult for a girl in junior high to be taken seriously if her body is still the size and shape of a fifth grader. And, unfortunately, images in magazines and on television show adolescent girls who are sexy from head to toe, slender but tall and well developed. Not only are these images unrealistic in general, they are totally out of sight for girls who are still waiting to hit puberty.

Being less developed than your friends can feel very isolating, like you can't relate to what's going on with them. If you are on the small side, and still waiting for your legs to lengthen and your breasts to grow, have no fear! Puberty begins anywhere from around age eight to age 14! If you have always been small or your family has a history of late puberty, chances are your body is developing in its own time and own special way.

While you have no control over how quickly or slowly your body matures, you do have control over how mature your behavior is. If you are frustrated, talk about it. Don't let your feelings build up like Sarah did; you may just end up pitching a fit like a little girl—which would only make you look more like a little girl! Show people that you may look young, but you have the ability to handle situations, responsibilities, and problems in a mature way.

Get Healthy

1. Make a list of things you like about yourself that have nothing to do with your size.

2. Develop a cool hobby, such as learning to play the guitar.

3. Remember—everyone develops in her own time and own way.

4. Talk to your parents about how you feel when they don't take you seriously.

The Last Word from Ashley

Girls who still look very young and underdeveloped may worry that they aren't developing properly or that something is wrong with them. Some girls might even worry that they will never develop!

They shouldn't worry—developing later is perfectly normal. In fact, it may be a good thing. Girls who develop later are not rushed into adulthood as early as other girls. When their bodies do develop, they will be older and more emotionally ready to participate in more adult activities.

4

The Early Bird

While the late bloomer may feel as though no one pays attention to her, the "early bird" may wish that people paid less attention to her. The sexiness of women's bodies is valued very highly in our culture. As a result, a girl whose body develops into adulthood earlier than most of her peers often receives much more attention than the less-developed girls.

Older boys may begin to notice her, or boys her own age may act differently toward her than they did before she developed. Girls her own age may become jealous of the attention she receives for her body. Sometimes vicious sexual rumors will be spread about her. At the same time, she may notice her parents acting strangely uncomfortable around their newly "grown-up" daughter.

All of the strong reactions the "early bird" experiences can result in a mix of emotions. Her body is the source of both positive and negative attention. She may find herself flattered and ashamed at the same time.

Aisha's Story

Aisha had always looked older than other girls her age. She was tall, and her body began to get small curves when she was ten years old, the same year she had her first period. But even with her period and developing body, looking older had never really bothered Aisha. In fact, her height had helped her become a strong athlete and earn respect easily. She was used to being in charge. She tried not to be too bossy, but she was willing to raise her voice for what she felt was right. It was her confident and fair attitude that had won Aisha the role of captain of the basketball team in the seventh grade.

Aisha began to get small curves when she was ten years old.

That same year, Aisha's breasts, which already were bigger than any of the girls on her team, grew from a size 32B to a size 34D. They felt heavy and awkward

when she ran during basketball practice. It didn't help that her hips had gotten wider, and she wasn't running as fast as before. Aisha always had been cool and in control, but all of a sudden her big breasts made her uncomfortable. Looking around at her teammates, she felt more like the coach than the captain.

Aisha tried hard to hide her big chest by wearing an extra tank top over her bra and loose shirts, but her large chest was still noticeable. The boys in her neighborhood even started to make comments when they played games outside after school. They'd always acted like she was one of them because she could run fast and play ball. But all of a sudden, they started to tell her she was sexy and asked to touch her. She pretended not to care, rolling her eyes and telling them to shut up, but the comments bothered her.

Even at home, she felt weird. Her father didn't seem to want to hug her anymore, and her mother kept talking about how much she was "growing." She started feeling ashamed of her body and didn't like the fact that she was becoming a woman.

Talk About It

- **Have you ever felt like you couldn't relate to your peers because of the way that you looked?**
- **Have you ever felt ashamed or embarrassed by how your body was developing? How did you handle it?**

One time, a neighborhood boy who was a few years older stole a ball from Aisha and his hand actually rubbed up against her breast. He looked directly in her eyes when it happened, and Aisha felt her face flush red. A part of her was mad, but a part of her also kind of liked it. Aisha was flattered that he had chosen her as the one to touch. When she got up, she glared at the boy but walked away instead of saying anything. Later, she worried about what to say if it happened again. She didn't know what to do, so she stopped playing with the neighbor kids altogether.

Talk About It

- **Have your friends ever treated you differently because of the way you look? What did you do?**

- **Why did Aisha feel both happy and mad when the boy touched her breast?**

- **What does it mean that "he had chosen her to touch"?**

Some of the girls on Aisha's team started to spread rumors about different boys who supposedly had touched Aisha's breasts. When she heard the rumors, she wanted to hide from embarrassment. Again, she felt the pang of shame about her body. At the same time, she felt responsible. She felt that it was her fault when the older boy touched her because she had liked it. Aisha wondered secretly if she was dirty. She was so confused, and she knew she couldn't do anything about her body developing. For a long time, Aisha said nothing, hoping the rumors would go away.

Aisha said nothing, hoping the rumors would go away.

Talk About It

- Has anyone ever spread rumors about you? Have you ever spread them about other people?

- What would you do to stop untrue rumors that were being spread about you?

- How could you help Aisha if you were on her team and heard the rumors?

Over time, the rumors became worse. The girls were saying that Aisha was having sex with all the boys on the football team. Some even said she was having sex with teachers! This made her so upset that she visited her basketball coach, Miss Brown, and told her what was happening. Her coach listened to everything she said. Aisha even told her about the one boy who had touched her. Finally, after Aisha was finished talking, Miss Brown turned to her and said, "Well, what are we going to do about this?"

"I don't know. There's nothing I can do, I guess," Aisha said. "I don't think my teammates would listen to me."

"But they always follow your lead during practice," her coach pointed out. "I think the girls respect you when you speak up."

Aisha hadn't thought about it that way before. After all, basketball didn't have that much in common with breasts and sex rumors. But, she remembered all the times when she was able to get respect with her words. So Aisha decided to talk to everyone at the next practice.

She was nervous when she stood before her teammates that afternoon. She took a deep breath before she spoke.

"I want to talk to the team about something. People have been spreading nasty rumors about me just because my boobs are so big. I didn't have sex with anyone, and it really sucks to hear that people I thought were my friends would say that about me. How would you feel if that happened to you? We're supposed to be on the same team, not against each other."

She felt better almost immediately after she said it out loud. Pretty soon, the rumors stopped, and Aisha felt more comfortable at practice, at school, and even in her neighborhood.

Talk About It

- Do you think Aisha handled the situation in the right way? Are there other ways to deal with rumors?

- Do you think you could speak up for yourself like Aisha did?

- What do you think her friends did to make the rumors stop? Do you have friends who would stick up for you?

In middle school and junior high, girls sometimes turn against each other. Usually, girls talk badly about each other because they are insecure about themselves or jealous of another girl. A lot of girls worry that their bodies don't measure up to the images of curvy, big-breasted women. They might make fun of other girls as a way to take the pressure off themselves, even while they may secretly wish their own breasts would grow.

Girls who have adult-looking bodies often get accused of having adult behaviors, such as having sex at very young ages. Early Birds may feel violated or dirty when their bodies become the topic of public conversation. It is embarrassing when very private changes become so public.

During middle school, many girls start to have thoughts about kissing or touching. The "early bird" might feel guilty about those thoughts because she feels people already assume that she's sexually active. But, the truth is that it's normal for girls this age to start having feelings about boys, and even like it when boys touch them.

Get Healthy

1. Stick up for yourself. You don't have to be the captain of a team to get others' respect.

2. Have a game plan before something happens. Talk to your friends about what you would do if someone touched you without your permission. That way, you'll be more prepared if it happens.

3. Instead of joining in on gossip, get the facts.

4. Enjoy what you've got. There's not much you can do about your natural shape, so don't bother trying to cover it up.

The Last Word from Ashley

Just because a girl has a curvier body doesn't mean she's any more ready to become sexual. If a developed girl feels alone without the support of her friends, she may be more likely to try to use her body to get attention from boys or even men. This can put her in dangerous or unhealthy situations. Girls can help protect themselves and each other by not spreading rumors that can hurt or isolate other girls.

5

The
Misfit

American culture is becoming increasingly diverse. Greater numbers of people from all over the world impact the music we listen to, the food we eat, and the way we speak and dress. There might be two girls in the same class who love the same hip-hop song, but one of them wears jeans to school every day while the other one dresses in hijab. Tons of kids who speak English at school also speak another language, such as Polish, Korean, or Spanish, with their families at home.

Even though it probably would be weird to see a classroom filled with kids from only one racial background than 11, it still is not easy for anyone who sees herself as an outsider. Girls whose customs are very different from their peers may find it hard to fit in. It can be even harder for girls of mixed race because they aren't sure which group they belong to. For these girls, finding good role models can be especially difficult. They may begin to resent their so-called "exotic" appearance and wish that they fit into a single category.

Judy's Story

Judy was 13 when her family moved from the city to the suburbs outside Chicago. She had plenty of friends in the city, and they would shop, go to movies, and get mochas at coffee shops. Judy was funny and bubbly. But at her new school in the suburbs, she felt like she had no one to talk to.

Judy was a combination of Chinese, African-American, and white. That had never seemed to matter in Chicago, where groups of kids from different backgrounds all hung out with each other. But here it seemed like everyone had his or her own group. It was as if the tables in the cafeteria had labels that said "White," "Asian," "Black," and "Mexican." On the first day, Judy had no idea where to sit, so she ate alone.

It was as if the tables in the cafeteria had labels that said "White," "Asian," "Black," and "Mexican." On the first day, Judy had no idea where to sit, so she ate alone.

Judy knew that her parents moved so that she could attend a better school to help her get into college one day. So, she tried not to let it bother her that she was alone all the time. Once, she tried to strike up a conversation with a group of Korean girls, but they kept looking at each other as if she wasn't there. Another time she asked a white girl if she wanted to be partners in biology class, but the girl said she already had a partner.

When Judy got home from school, she looked at herself in the mirror. With light caramel skin, coarse, kinky hair, and almond-shaped eyes, people often complimented Judy for being pretty. At her new school, however, she felt ugly and untouchable. None of the boys looked her way. In fact, no one looked at her much at all. She started to wish that she looked less unusual so she could fit in with at least one of the groups at school.

At her new school, Judy felt ugly and untouchable.

Judy was really homesick for her old school and begged her parents to move back to Chicago, but they refused. For a few months she talked to and instant messaged her old friends every day. While she was talking to them, she felt like she still was part of everything. But when they hung up or signed off, she felt even more lost and lonely.

Talk About It

- **How important do you think it is that there are other kids at your school who share a similar ethnic background?**

- **Are you the only one in your school of a particular race, religion, or mixed ethnic group? How does that make you feel?**

Eventually, Judy didn't feel like she was a part of her old circle either. She began to spend time talking to people on the Internet she'd never met. She would make up profiles with fake descriptions of herself, such as "tall with blond hair and blue eyes" or "black and athletic." Anything else seemed to fit together better than "Asian, black, and white."

Talk About It

- Could reasons other than Judy's appearance be making it harder for her to find friends?

- Can you think of a time that you felt like you had to look like everyone else to have friends? How did you feel about it?

Sometimes the friends Judy met online felt almost the same as friends in real life, until she remembered that they had no idea who she really was. And that made her feel even worse.

Judy missed hanging out with "real" people and having "real" friends. And she really missed just being herself—in person and online.

Talk About It

- Are online friends the same as friends you meet in person?

- What are some good and bad things about meeting people on the Internet?

- Have you ever made up a profile for yourself? What happened? How did you feel?

Ask Dr. Vicki

No matter what background they come from, most girls go through a period when they worry that they don't belong because of the way that they look. Some girls try to re-create new identities to fit into a particular idea of what they think they should look like. Most of the time, trying to be something you're not will only make you feel worse about yourself.

It is important to remember that even when you feel like you are the only person who doesn't fit in, a lot of other girls feel the same way. Even though our culture is becoming more accepting of people from different backgrounds, we still have a tendency to group people together based on their race, religion, how much money they have, or what language they speak. It can take time to appreciate how special having a diverse family and racial background makes you.

Get Healthy

1. Focus on what things you have in common with other students, rather than what's different.

2. Get involved in an after-school activity. Finding common interests is one way to fit in. If you're on the same team as other people, it will be easier to accept each other.

3. Talk to your parents about where you come from. Ask them what it was like for them when they were growing up.

4. Try to see the beauty in each individual part of yourself instead of worrying about how it looks to other people.

5. Try to comment on another student's difference in a positive way (such as her hairstyle or clothes).

6. Limit the time you spend online. Meeting people online can be fun, but in the long run you will feel closer to the friends you can talk to in person.

The Last Word from Ashley

Luckily, our ideas of beauty are changing. Mixed-race girls are becoming valued more for their unique beauty and not excluded as often because they don't fit into a mold. Still, the way that a girl thinks and feels is more important than the way that she looks. Even though it can be hard to feel like an outsider, many times girls like to stand out in a crowd when they get to be older. Many mixed-race girls eventually feel proud of their unusual look.

6

The Tomboy

Being more or less developed than the other girls at school can be difficult, especially if you don't want to stand out. A lot of girls wish their bodies looked more like the other, more feminine girls. But, plenty of girls prefer a more casual, less girly style. They also may be more interested in sports or other activities usually thought of as boy stuff. Sometimes called "tomboys," these girls don't have much interest in dressing or acting like a typical girl.

Even though they may not be interested in the activities girls their age are "supposed" to be interested in, that doesn't mean that they are purposely trying to stand out. They want to be accepted in school and have a good group of friends just as much as the next girl. They just want to do it on their own terms.

So how does a girl gain acceptance and respect without acting or dressing like every other girl? How can a girl be cool and feel cute and comfortable in her own skin but keep the boyish, athletic style that she likes? And, how does a girl who dresses like a boy deal with accusations or assumptions about her sexuality? What if she likes boys but is afraid to show it? What if she likes other girls as more than friends?

How does a girl gain acceptance and respect without dressing like every other girl?

These are big questions that a lot of girls start to think about during the middle school years. Read on to learn how Jen lived through it.

Jen's Story

Jen wasn't always called Jen. When she was very small, her parents named her Jennifer. Later, when she started school, people shortened her name to Jenny. In the middle of eighth grade, she decided that she would rather be called Jen.

It started with a button-down shirt. Jen had always been a "tomboy," and before junior high no one seemed to care. But then, button-down shirts became popular, and everything seemed to change.

Everyone in eighth grade wanted cotton button-down shirts from the same store at the mall. They were simple shirts in a variety of colors, with three buttons at the top. Jen wanted one too. They were comfortable cotton and looked good with jeans. When she went to the store to get one, she saw the shirt in pink, light yellow, and baby blue on one side of the store. She frowned when she noticed that even the large size looked tight enough to fit a ten-year-old. Jen liked loose and baggy shirts that she could move around in. She couldn't understand why other girls wanted to wear them so tight.

Then she noticed the boy version on the other side of the store. They were bigger and came in gray, navy blue, or black, some of Jen's favorite colors. She bought two because she couldn't decide on a color and wore one to school the next day. A bunch of other kids had the shirts, so Jen wasn't surprised that some of the boys were wearing the same color shirts as hers. She saw girls with the pink and light blue versions too. Since Jen was a "tomboy," her clothes didn't always fit in. She was glad that she was wearing the right thing for once.

At least, that's how she felt until she got home to her older brother. John took one look at Jen's shirt and laughed. "You're such a dyke," he said. "Look at my little sister, the lesss-bian!" This wasn't the first time Jen's brother had called her names, and he often accused her of wanting to kiss her girlfriends. But for some reason, it bothered Jen more this time than it had in the past.

Talk About It

- **Why do you think John's comment bothered Jen this time more than other times?**

- **If a girl likes to wear boys' clothes, does that mean she's gay? If a girl wears girly clothes, is that proof that she likes boys?**

- **Has anyone ever called you gay because of how you dress?**

Jen looked down at her new shirt, which she had liked so much earlier that day. Suddenly she felt ashamed. She was embarrassed for wearing boys' clothes, but she hated wearing girls' clothes. She worried sometimes that she was a lesbian just as her brother said. She knew she wasn't attracted to other girls, but she didn't like boys in that way either.

Jen was embarrassed for wearing boys' clothes, but she hated wearing girls' clothes.

Talk About It

- **How can a person know whether he or she is gay? Have you ever wondered if you were gay?**

- **What advice would you give Jen?**

Jen continued to wear her new shirts. She liked the way she looked in them, cool and laid-back. Still, every time she wore them, she worried that people would think she was trying to be a boy.

Her female friends tried to get her to borrow their dresses or other girly clothes sometimes. They'd say, "You'd look so much cuter if you would just dress like a girl." Sometimes she would do it just so they would stop bothering her, but she wished people didn't care so much about how she looked.

Talk About It

- Why does everyone care what Jen wears?

- How do you think Jen feels when other people try to get her to dress more girly?

- Has anyone ever tried to get you to dress in a different style? How did it feel?

After a while, Jen stopped wearing her friends' clothes. She was sick of feeling like a little kid in a costume. Sometimes Jen felt weird when she was around a group of pretty girls. She just didn't understand what all the fuss was about. Most of the time, she was more comfortable in her boyish jeans and T-shirts.

Girls who reject their girlishness often struggle between two wrongs. On one hand, it feels wrong and uncomfortable to wear girly clothing. On the other hand, people tell them they are wrong when they wear boys' clothing or refuse to take on a girlish outward appearance. These girls may wonder why their feelings fail to match what other people say is right. Such a girl may have self-doubt or feelings of failure because she is not a boy but also not totally a girl. She is somewhere in between.

Most adolescent girls are somewhat unsure about their feelings regarding sex. So, it is especially challenging for "tomboys" when their sexuality is called into question. These girls may be forced to answer questions about their sexual feelings before any of their classmates.

"Tomboys" may find that their parents buy them pink things and offer to get their hair styled or nails done. Sometimes these girls feel that they aren't measuring up—that their parents want a girly girl. If you are afraid that you are somehow disappointing your parents, tell them how you feel. They may be surprised to find out how their offers are being perceived. An important part of being who you are is learning to speak up if you feel misunderstood.

Get Healthy

1. Make a list of all the people you look up to and respect and why. You will see that the way they dress doesn't have a lot to do with how you feel about them.

2. Get involved in coed group activities. Look for opportunities to be part of a team. Youth groups can be a good source for coed fun.

3. Don't keep your questions and fears bottled up inside. Find a trusted adult (parent, other relative, teacher, religious leader, youth group adviser, or a friend's mother) to share your feelings with and find answers to your questions.

The Last Word from Ashley

Almost everyone is trying to figure out who they are in middle school. "Tomboys" are too, except they may have people constantly questioning them. "What are you?" or "Are you gay?" are among the questions they may face. There is a bright side, though. These girls may have more friends of both genders. Boys actually might feel more comfortable with a girl who isn't trying to get him to ask her out. And, girls may like being around a girl who isn't trying to compete for a boyfriend. Some "tomboys" also have a tendency to develop strong leadership skills over time because they are used to being very independent.

7

The
Freak

When people talk about body image, they often forget to talk about disability. Instead, disabilities get put in a category with prejudice and discrimination. Surely, people with disabilities at any age are discriminated against when working, using public transportation, or going out to eat or to the movies. What people forget to talk about is how having a disability can affect an adolescent girl's feelings about her body.

Girls with disabilities face big hurdles to being accepted by their peers. A lot of kids are so worried about fitting in and looking cool that they are afraid to be friends with someone who will stand out. Within the cold halls of a typical middle school, a girl with even a minor speech problem, like a lisp, easily can be made to feel like she's from another planet. Other kids might be outright rude, making cruel jokes at her expense. They might ignore her altogether. Other times, they might be friendly out of pity. Plus, girls with disabilities often have to face the fact that their differences from other girls are permanent. Any way you cut it, a girl with a disability is likely to feel impossibly different from her classmates.

On the flip side, the knowledge that her body isn't perfect gives a disabled girl the upper hand in a way. After all, everyone has problems in their lives sooner or later. Girls with any sort of disability may be able to accept themselves for who they are earlier than other girls because they know that most things related to the body are out of their control.

Girls with disabilities often have to face the fact that their differences from other girls are permanent.

Jackie's Story

Jackie was really smart. She usually beat everyone at board games and could answer random trivia questions better than anyone else she knew. Jackie also had a disability. When she was born, Jackie was diagnosed with a medical condition that made one side of her body seem like it was asleep. Her speech was badly affected, and she kind of dragged one leg when she walked.

Jackie went to physical therapy and speech classes while other kids were at soccer practice or taking piano lessons. It felt natural to her, except when other people treated her like a freak. Unfortunately, this happened more often than she cared to think about. It took her longer to speak full sentences, and certain words were impossible to say at all. For that reason, Jackie hardly spoke to anyone at school except her best friend, Becka.

Talk About It

- **What does it mean to be "treated like a freak"?**

- **Have you ever felt like a freak?**

- **Has anyone ever called you a freak or treated you like one?**

Becka and Jackie first became friends in fourth grade, when they had assigned seats next to each other. Becka was shy and didn't have a lot of friends either. For two years, Becka and Jackie spent all their free time together, playing games and watching movies. Becka also was the only person at school with whom Jackie could talk about her disability. When she got down in the dumps, Becka could cheer her up, saying, "You know I don't even think about it or notice it anymore."

Even though Becka was pretty, she never acted like she was better than Jackie, and when they were together, Jackie felt more normal.

Becka and Jackie usually consoled each other when it came to school social events, such as dances or ball games. When the spring dance approached, Becka and Jackie made fun of the girls who were buying dresses months before the dance. They joked about crashing the dance dressed as barn animals. They both knew that they would be spending the evening at one of their houses, watching their most recent favorite movie for the tenth time.

Two weeks before the day of the dance, Becka and Jackie were eating lunch in the cafeteria when Becka announced that she had been asked to go. Jackie felt a chill run down her spine.

"Who is it?" she asked.

"Travis Daley. He sent me a text in chorus this morning."

"Well you're not going to go, right? I mean, you're going to sleep over at my house like always, right?"

"Well, I don't know. It might be fun, you know, to go . . ." Becka's voice trailed off.

"But what will I do?" Jackie demanded. She didn't like the pleading she could hear in her voice, but she couldn't help herself.

Jackie knew by the look on Becka's face that she would be watching movies alone on the night of the dance.

Talk About It

• **Why did Jackie feel a chill run down her spine? How would you react if you were Jackie?**

The next week, Becka had to buy a dress for the dance. Jackie teased her a little but ended up going with her to the mall anyway since she had nothing better to do. Becka tried on a fitted black dress. It was exactly the dress Jackie would have chosen if she didn't feel so weird in dressy clothes. Standing next to Becka in the dressing room, Jackie couldn't help but compare their reflections. She winced at her own slightly droopy mouth. Who would ever want to dance with her or kiss her when she looked so ugly?

Talk About It

- Is it fair that Jackie doesn't want Becka to go to the dance? How do you think Jackie is feeling? What about Becka?

- Have you ever wanted to keep a friend from doing something because you felt left out? How did you handle the situation?

- Is Jackie worried about just the dance, or could there be something more bothering her?

Jackie was so miserable about the idea of being alone on the night of the dance, and possibly all the dances for the rest of her life, that she started to ignore Becka. In turn, Becka was even more quiet than usual. After dropping Becka off one day, Jackie's mom asked, "What is going on with you two?" Jackie decided to tell her mom the story about the dance.

Standing next to Becka in the dressing room, Jackie couldn't help but compare their reflections.

"It's not fair that she gets to go and I can't. What if Becka starts going to dances all the time, and I am the ugly one stuck at home? I will never be able to go to dances without looking like an ugly freak."

"I know it's hard to feel left out, but Becka is a really good friend to you," her mom said. "I think if you want to keep her as a friend, you have to let her know it's okay that you don't always have to do the same things all the time. Otherwise she might start to resent you."

Jackie was not prepared for her mom's response. She thought her mom would feel bad for her and re-assure her that she wasn't ugly. She wished she could be reassured that she wasn't ugly and believe it. She hated the idea of being alone and unwanted. At the same time, she realized that she didn't want to push her best friend away just because she was feeling bad about herself. She took a deep breath and picked up the phone to call Becka.

Talk About It

- **What do you think Jackie is going to tell Becka?**

- **How do you think Jackie will feel staying home without Becka the night of the dance?**

- **Have you ever felt left out? What advice could you give to Jackie?**

Jackie's insecurities about her appearance and her physical limitations almost came between her and her best friend. Luckily her mother helped her see the big picture and do the right thing.

Like Jackie, some girls with disabilities feel that life has been unfair to them. They feel that it is more difficult to make friends and have the chance to let people know who they really are. Because of this struggle, they may develop only a few close friendships. And given that the number of friends is so limited, they may become clingy, demanding, or possessive to hold on to them. However, if they accept that their friends may want to have other relationships as well, their friendships can be long lasting.

If you find yourself trying to hold on too tightly to a friend, you might squash the friendship altogether. Making one person the center of your world is not healthy. If your friend wants to pursue other relationships or interests, you could, too. They may just need to be with different people or different groups. Then when you get together, you can share your various experiences with each other. You might find that you actually have more to talk about!

Get Healthy

1. Don't be a shut-in. Take advantage of facilities and resources at your school and in your community to help you be a part of sports teams or participate in other activities.

2. Realize that people are afraid of what they don't understand. Work on talking about your disability. If you are ashamed or uncomfortable about it, other people will pick up on that. But if you're okay with it, other people might be more okay with it, too.

3. Get involved in activities that provide accommodations for certain disabilities. Ask your parents, teachers, or doctors about groups and activities geared for kids experiencing the same kinds of challenges you are. This will help you feel like others understand what you're going through.

The Last Word from Ashley

Whether it's a crooked mouth or a shorter leg, a hearing aid or thick glasses, it is important to remember that your disability doesn't define who you are! It is only one of the many aspects that make you the wonderful person that you truly are. Help people see past the disability by letting your beautiful qualities shine through. Get involved in activities where your talents can soar and find groups that accept you as you are.

8

The Pizza Face

Skin is a big deal during adolescence. With hormones going in every direction, almost all kids get zits, also called acne. Lots of kids get zits all over their face, and others even get them all over their bodies. Acne can cause girls to become very self-conscious and embarrassed. Tons of other skin-related problems can cause anxiety too, such as having abnormally dry skin, a big birthmark, or a noticeable scar.

When skin problems become a major issue, it can be difficult to focus on anything else—including priorities like schoolwork. Like a lot of body stuff, you can't always do very much about your skin. Girls with chronic acne are often mortified and will go to great measures to try to conceal it. Unfortunately, sometimes makeup can irritate skin and cause more pimples. And the more you worry about your skin, the worse it tends to get. Casey confronted this very problem.

Casey's Story

Casey learned the hard way how important it is not to get so worked up about her face when she nearly failed math class because of her zits. Casey returned to school for sixth grade with new blemishes on her chin and forehead. It seemed she was constantly breaking out no matter how often she washed her face. She became horrified that despite all the products she tried, her skin was becoming bumpier, redder, and oilier.

Girls with chronic acne are often mortified and will go to great measures to try to conceal it.

Between classes, and especially during the long break after lunch, Casey would retreat to the girls' bathroom. She tried not to pick at her skin, but she often did anyway, leaving red marks that she then would try to cover with heavy makeup.

That year, Casey was enrolled in Mr. Goularas's Advanced Math class. She had been chosen for the class because she had gotten such a high score on the

math section of the standard test she'd taken in fifth grade. A quick problem solver, Casey had been excited to move into the advanced class. But, Casey's concerns about her skin soon took precedence over her interest in math. She spent so much time in the bathroom that she was regularly late for class and had trouble concentrating on her schoolwork. While in class, she hid behind her book and tried to cover up the red marks she got from picking at her skin.

Casey began to feel lost and inadequate in class. Instead of working with her teacher to catch up, she worried more about her acne and blamed it for her slipping grades. By the end of the first term, Casey was on the verge of receiving a D in Advanced Math. She knew if her grade went below a C-minus, she would not be able to move on to the next section with her classmates.

Finally, Mr. Goularas asked Casey to stay after class. He questioned her on why the term was going so poorly. He even asked if something was going on at home that could be causing her grade to slip. Casey thought about telling Mr. Goularas about her skin problems. But she was afraid he might think she was silly. Instead, she promised to work harder and do some extra credit to catch up.

Talk About It

- **Why does Casey think Mr. Goularas will think she is silly? Would you tell Mr. Goularas the truth if you were Casey?**

- **Is it fair for Casey to blame her acne for her slipping grades?**

- **Have you ever blamed body flaws for poor grades or forgotten homework?**

After Casey talked to Mr. Goularas, she began to think back to fifth grade, when she looked forward to math class and liked to laugh with her classmates. It seemed like so long ago, and she missed it. She remembered when what she saw on the chalkboard had nothing to do with what she saw in the mirror.

Talk About It

- Have you ever had embarrassing skin problems? What did you do?

- Have you ever allowed insecurity about your body to interfere with your ability to have fun or concentrate? What happened?

Casey started to realize how much time she was spending worrying about her skin. She had been so obsessed with her face that she had forgotten about what was underneath. She decided to try to pretend everything was the same as before she had skin problems. She stopped going to the bathroom so often in between classes and focused more on what her teacher was saying. She did extra math problems and concentrated on her assignments. She tried to smile more and stand up straighter. Finally, she did her best to

After months of feeling so self-conscious, Casey was amazed at how quickly she felt better.

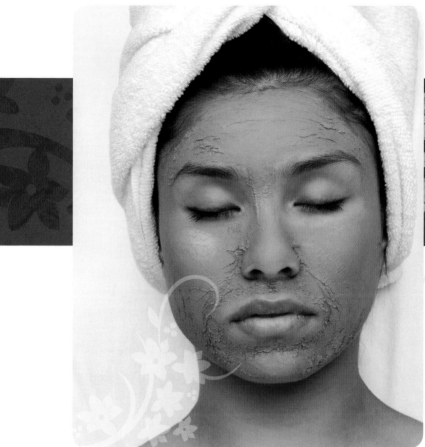

push out negative thoughts about her skin when they crept in.

After months of feeling so self-conscious, Casey was amazed at how quickly she felt better. With hard work, her math grade improved enough for her to pass with a C, and she vowed to do better during the second term. She even noticed her skin starting to clear up a bit after she stopped picking at it in the bathroom during the school day.

When insecurity starts to affect your personality, relationships, or schoolwork, it is a problem that needs to be addressed. Casey became so focused on her skin that she actually made the situation worse. Not only did her skin problems worsen, but her grades suffered, as well.

It is understandable that she wanted to have nice skin. Sometimes, we focus so much on a problem that it starts to seem bigger than it really is. Have you ever had a zit on your face and felt as though everyone was staring at it? All day long you might be worried more about that one zit than your math test or history lecture. Well, that's what Casey did; she became so focused on her skin that she lost sight of other things.

How did she make it better? She stopped focusing so much on it! She started looking at the big picture, shifted her focus, and worked on her attitude. By taking control of the situation, she proved to herself that she didn't have to let her skin condition control her thoughts and attention.

If you find yourself becoming fixated on a certain problem, talk to someone. If you are worried about your skin, check out the quality of the foods you eat, the cleansing you do, and the amount of exercise and sleep you get. Believe it or not, these habits can help with skin care a whole lot more than picking, squeezing, and rubbing. You can also make an appointment with your doctor to talk about skin care solutions.

Get Healthy

1. Check with a doctor before using products or taking medication for your skin.

2. Remember that most skin problems lessen over time. Be patient.

3. Take warm baths with soothing natural ingredients in your bubble bath. Ask your doctor about herbs that are safe for your skin.

4. Wear comfortable, non-itchy fabrics such as cotton. You'll feel pretty and you won't irritate your skin.

The Last Word from Ashley

Whether they are worried about zits or wrinkles, women face anxiety related to skin issues throughout their lives. Unfortunately, if a woman lets her worries get the better of her, she can spend a lot of money on products and a lot of time obsessing over flaws she will never be able to fix. It sounds simple, but practicing healthy habits such as eating a balanced diet and getting regular exercise can do wonders for the skin.

9

The Lame Dresser

There is one problem that all girls, no matter how pretty, ugly, fat, or thin they feel, will experience at some point. This problem is called, "not having anything to wear." Staying on top of trends can be tricky and costly, especially if you don't know what you're looking for or don't have the body or the budget to fit whatever is in style. It doesn't help that trends seem to change from one minute to the next, so the jeans you begged your mom to buy for you in the fall can seem so yesterday by spring.

At the same time, clothes can be a lot of fun. How girls dress is a major way that they express their personalities, show their interests, and identify which groups they belong to. Shopping and getting dressed often are social opportunities to hang out with your friends.

Because what you wear can be so important to whether other people think you're pretty or ugly, cool or dorky, it can be difficult if you don't have the right clothes. Kids judge each other by their wardrobes throughout junior high and high school. So what if you're the girl who's not invited to the party because you don't have the right shoes? Read Selena's story to find out how she handled that very situation.

Selena's Story

Selena was the third child in a family of six kids. With two brothers and three sisters, family life was always exciting, but the money was pretty tight. She and her brothers and sisters shared bedrooms and passed around a lot of hand-me-downs. There were even a few T-shirts that had been worn by all six of them at one time or another. Selena's mom always

Selena and her brothers and sisters passed around a lot of hand-me-downs.

kept all the kids showered and dressed in freshly laundered clothes, but the clothes sometimes lost the clean look because they'd been worn and washed so many times.

On the first day of sixth grade, Selena wanted to look extra nice, so she wore her sister Maria's red shirt from last season, a new pair of jeans from the sale rack at a local discount department store, and shoes that once belonged to her mother. Even though they were really old, she liked them because she thought they looked kind of cool and vintage. She had seen some in a similar retro style at one of the cooler stores in the mall. To top off her look, she wore her hair down and borrowed some of Maria's lip gloss. Checking herself out in the big living room mirror, she thought she looked pretty good. Maybe it wasn't the coolest outfit, but it definitely wasn't the lamest.

Talk About It

- Have you ever had to figure out what to wear to look cool? How did you solve the problem?

- In what ways was Selena creative and resourceful in selecting her outfit?

Most of the day was pretty uneventful. Selena saw friends from her neighborhood and said hi to last year's teachers. During English class, the students were asked to partner up for a project. Selena turned to smile at Patricia, who was sitting next to her. They'd been friendly the year before. To Selena's surprise, Patricia pretended she didn't see her and turned to wave at a girl in the back of the room. Embarrassed, Selena looked around for another partner and ended up with a dorky boy.

Talk About It

- How do you think it felt when Patricia ignored Selena? Why did she do that?
- Has someone ever ignored you? How did you feel and what did you do about it?

Throughout the rest of the period, Selena couldn't concentrate. She tried to figure out why Patricia had ignored her. Then she thought about Lorena, the girl Patricia had chosen instead. Lorena had perfectly cut hair with a style like the star actress on a popular television show. Her jeans showed the designer label above the back pocket, and she had another big brand label across her chest. All the makeup she wore and the expensive handbag she carried to class made her look at least a year older than Selena.

Right then, Selena decided that Patricia had chosen Lorena because she looked cool. Selena felt stupid in the outfit she'd worked so hard to pick out that morning. Suddenly Selena hated her clothes.

She hated the color of her shirt, the shape of her jeans, and her ratty old shoes. There was no way this outfit could ever compare to what Lorena was wearing.

Talk About It

- Have you ever decided that you hated something you were wearing even though you had liked it before? What made you change your mind?

- How does it feel to compare yourself to another girl?

In the following days, Selena did her best to wear the plainest, least noticeable clothes possible. She knew she didn't look any cooler, but she hoped that she at least looked like she didn't care and wasn't trying. This approach worked for a while—Selena didn't worry about Patricia or Lorena making fun of her behind her back. Sometimes on the weekends, one of Selena's friends would let her borrow a jacket or a pair of sneakers if they thought boys would be around. Selena appreciated being able to borrow her friends' clothes, but she always felt a twinge of sadness when she had to return them at the end of the night. Selena longed for a style and clothing that were her own.

Sick of trying to make herself invisible or borrowing her friends' stuff, Selena started looking around her house for things to wear. With such a big family, she had a lot of clothes to go through, but most of the items weren't wearable. Finally she found some boxes with her mom's old dresses and suits and even a pair of shoes in the same style as the shoes Selena had worn to school on the first day. Selena really liked something about these old clothes. The dresses were pretty and colorful but looked way different from the stuff Selena's classmates wore. When she tried them on, she felt glamorous and beautiful as she imagined her mother had looked when she'd worn them back in the day.

Sick of trying to make herself invisible or borrowing her friends' stuff, Selena started looking around her house for things to wear.

Talk About It

- **Have you ever shared clothes with your friends? Who did the borrowing, you or them?**

- **Do you like sharing clothes? Why or why not?**

- **Have you ever tried to put together an outfit from old clothing? Did you like what it looked like?**

Then Selena remembered how beautiful her mom always seemed—and it wasn't about her clothes. Her mom was strong, confident, and determined. She had a great sense of humor and a style that was all her own. Selena smiled.

She started mixing and matching pieces and wearing the old clothes to school. At first she was nervous that people would think she was weird, but then a few boys from her class said her outfits were "the bomb." Selena knew that not everyone would love her new look, but she didn't care so much because it felt like her own.

Talk About It

- What does it mean that Selena's look "felt like her own"? Why does this make her care less about other people's opinions?

- Can you think of a time when you went against what was popular and did your own thing? How did it feel?

Finding a personal style can be a major process for some girls. On one hand, it seems so important to fit in but on the other hand, girls also want to show who they are and how they are unique. Even girls who want to wear a brand label may want to wear it in their own way. Selena did an awesome job of finding ways to wear the clothes that were available to her. Instead of continuing to feel like she didn't measure up to the other girls, she did her own thing.

Not all girls will be as brave as Selena about their clothing choices. Having other body image issues, like being overweight or hating one's hair, can make girls even less likely to try to stand out. But even if a girl is not willing to wear an outfit from another era to school, she may be willing to add her own personal touches to plain clothes to help her feel proud of her look.

Get Healthy

1. Make your own jewelry or other accessory, like a belt. Tons of Web sites and books teach you how to be crafty on the cheap.

2. Keep the clothes that you like wearing, even if they go out of style. Over time you may find that keeping up with every trend is not as important as feeling comfortable.

3. When you shop for new clothes, ask yourself if you really like something, or if you're only buying it to fit in. Most trendy clothes will end up in the giveaway pile eventually.

4. Recycling old clothes or making new clothes out of old material is a cool way to get an interesting look and do something good for the environment at the same time.

The Last Word from Ashley

As much as having the right clothes can make a girl feel like she belongs to a group, the fact that trends change so quickly can be stressful for girls as they try to fit in and develop personal style. Girls might find that they have even more fun finding creative ways to put their outfits together, instead of buying everything right off the mannequin.

Plus, if you find a look that doesn't cost as much, you can spend money on other things, like music or books. You don't have to be confined to the mall to look and feel cool.

10

The Stick Figure

Most women and girls are well aware of how much pressure they are under to look good. It is no easy feat to feel good about our bodies. Many body image issues can affect girls' self-image during adolescence. But, it is possible to make positive choices to feel better and more in control.

Still, many other girls will not make such healthy choices. Take Lindsey, who ate far too little for weeks only to eat an entire box of cookies after being teased for being fat. This probably is a very realistic example of how a girl who is worried about her weight might handle her pain and feelings of self-hate. Yo-yo diets like Lindsey's have become all too common among adolescent girls. Some experts say that most girls have dieted before they've even started middle school.

The dieting and fashion industries are part of the problem. Advertisements for new diets and fashion continuously send the message that being thin is equal to being healthy and beautiful. But, our cultural obsession with

Dieting at a young age puts girls at risk for serious eating disorders, such as anorexia and bulimia.

thin bodies actually is extremely harmful to adolescent girls. Dieting at a young age puts girls at risk for serious eating disorders, such as anorexia and bulimia.

Anorexia and bulimia probably are the most common and well-known of eating disorders. Anorexia is a disorder in which a person, usually an adolescent girl or adult woman, literally starves herself and refuses to maintain the lowest minimum weight for her height and age. Doctors usually identify a girl who skips three or more menstrual periods in a row as "medically anorexic."

Girls who suffer from bulimia often restrict their food intake like anorexics but also will binge and purge. This means they will eat a large amount of food at one time, then force themselves to throw it up to avoid gaining weight. Some bulimics will exercise excessively or take laxatives to get rid of food calories. Most girls

with eating disorders engage in a combination of anorexic and bulimic behaviors in an effort to be thin.

With all the horrible health problems this behavior can cause, it's surprising that the number of girls
with eating disorders is actually growing. But the sad

truth is, more and more girls are risking their health, and even their lives, to be thin. Why are girls so dead set on being thin? Is it because they believe being thin will make them happy or successful? What can you do to protect yourself and your friends from developing an eating disorder?

Audrey's Story

Audrey wasn't always a stick figure. She used to look normal, athletic, and healthy. Audrey had been one of the best swimmers on the swim team. With her strong legs and competitive spirit, she won several competitions. She also performed in school plays. Audrey considered herself to be pretty. Her parents always told her she was, although sometimes her mother suggested certain exercises that might help Audrey keep her butt and legs from becoming "too beefy." Audrey did sometimes feel self-conscious during swim meets because her butt and legs were thicker than some of the other girls'.

Midway through the swim season Audrey got bumped to the fast lane. She was the youngest person in her group and was proud that she had been chosen. On her first day with her new team, the coach said they would have to work especially hard and be extra disciplined to win the championship that year. Audrey took the speech to heart and began practicing longer hours every day to improve. Some of the other girls on her team followed a high-protein diet to stay trim and swim faster, so Audrey started it too. Even though she loved chocolate, she cut out all desserts.

At first, Audrey's swimming seemed to improve quickly with all the extra hours she put into it. She also noticed her body becoming more toned. Some of the other girls on her team commented that she looked thinner. One girl even said she was jealous of Audrey's body. Feeling proud of herself, Audrey decided to cut back on the fats in her diet as well. She stopped eating butter and cheese altogether, and would only allow herself to eat proteins, vegetables, and multigrain bread. By the time swim season ended, Audrey had lost almost 10 pounds (4.5 kg) since the beginning of the season. She had dropped an entire size in jeans.

Even though the season was over, Audrey decided to keep up her diet. She told herself she was doing it to prepare for next year, but in truth she liked how it felt to eat less. She was very careful about making sure her portions were small so she never felt full. The lightness in her stomach made her feel more energetic. Her mom also had

Even though the season was over, Audrey decided to keep up her diet. She liked how it felt to eat less.

taken her shopping for clothes in her new smaller size, and she wanted to make sure she stayed thin enough to wear them. Her mother was very proud of Audrey's new shape and mentioned almost every day how cute and fit she looked.

Talk About It

- Have you ever gone on a diet? Was it one of the latest fads? Did it work?

- What do you think about Audrey's diet? Is this healthy or unhealthy?

- How do you feel about Audrey's mother complimenting her daughter on her weight loss?

Audrey replaced swim practice with running every day. She made sure never to skip a workout and increased the miles she would run every few weeks. She knew she was losing more weight. She wasn't exactly trying to lose weight, but she was determined not to gain any. Every pound she lost set a new standard that she needed to maintain. Audrey started going on Web sites where girls shared diet secrets and found that she could skip meals if she drank a lot of water. She also read about a few girls who would eat when they got really hungry but then throw up the food so the calories wouldn't make them fat. That sounded kind of gross to Audrey, but she was curious if it really worked.

A few months after swim season ended, Audrey tried on a pair of shorts and couldn't believe she could fit into them. They were the size that the really skinny girls wore. She felt so pretty and thin that she smiled all the time and talked more at school. More boys started

to talk to her, and the older girls on the swim team invited her to parties.

At one particular sleepover, the girls ordered pizzas. Everyone was eating it, although some of the girls only ate one piece. Audrey didn't want to eat any of it. It made her a little sick to think about how greasy it was. These days, she never ate any processed fats and hardly ate any bread because she had read that carbs would make you puffy. But, she also didn't want to seem weird because she was the only one who wouldn't eat the pizza. So she picked up a piece and ate it very slowly, picking off most of the cheese and pepperoni. Later, she felt so guilty about eating the pizza that she snuck into a bathroom upstairs and put her fingers down her throat to throw it up.

Talk About It

- **Why does eating the pizza make Audrey feel guilty?**
- **What do you think of Audrey's decision to throw it up?**
- **Have you ever been in a situation where you decided to eat, drink, or do something in order to fit in? What did you do?**

After that night at the party, Audrey started to make herself throw up more often after she ate. She would do it a few times a week when she felt bad about eating something. Sometimes she would let herself eat something fatty or sugary because she knew she was going to puke it up immediately, but she mostly stuck to her super small portions and fat-free foods. Audrey became thinner and thinner. When she dropped to a size 2, she realized that she had lost almost 32 pounds (14.5 kg) in half a year.

Now that she weighed only 106 pounds (48.1 kg), it took all of Audrey's concentration to keep the weight off. She planned her meals days in advance. At the same time, she had very little appetite. Almost everything looked or tasted gross to her, but she would eat weird things, such as gobs of mustard, because it had no calories.

Audrey's parents started to become worried. They tried to get her to eat. Her mother started packing lunches for her that Audrey would throw away when she got to school. "I just don't want you to lose any more weight. You've lost enough," her mother would say. Audrey would think, "I've lost enough, but not too much. I can stay like this if I don't gain any weight."

Talk About It

- **What would you say to Audrey if you were her mother?**
- **How could you help Audrey if you were on her swim team?**

Still, the girls on Audrey's swim team told her all the time that they wished they were thin like she was. And, she lost more weight. Her hair started to become thin and dry. She was cold all the time. Her bones ached when she sat in one place for too long. Loud noises made her wince. She started to feel sad and uncomfortable. The only thing that made her feel better was looking at herself in the mirror and seeing how thin she was. Still, sometimes she looked in the mirror and thought she saw a roll of fat she'd never noticed before. Then she had to try harder to keep the weight off. She couldn't run as much anymore because she felt too weak, so she walked around constantly. She slept fitfully at night, sometimes dreaming of hot dogs or cake.

The only thing that made Audrey feel better was looking in the mirror and seeing how thin she was.

When Audrey's parents brought her to see the doctor, she weighed 94 pounds (42.6 kg). She looked like a little girl. She hadn't had a period for months. Her skin was gray, and her fingernails were blue. She was immediately diagnosed as anorexic and told that if she didn't start eating she could die. Audrey's mother cried. Audrey looked down, saying, "I don't have a problem. I'm just not as hungry as other people. I eat every day. I eat all the time. I must have a fast metabolism." Even as she said it, she knew she was lying. All of a sudden, Audrey felt her head spinning. She didn't want to be sick. What if they made her start eating? What if she got fat? Everyone said she was perfect. She was so tired of having to be perfect.

Talk About It

- **How do you think it feels to try to be perfect?**
- **Why do you think Audrey says she doesn't have a problem, even though she knows she is lying?**

Early detection is crucial to preventing eating disorders. It is especially important that mothers are positive and supportive of their daughters' bodies. Audrey's behavior was made worse by the attention and support she got from her mother and teammates for being thin. She wanted their approval.

Many girls with eating disorders find that others support and even encourage dangerous dieting until the problem becomes very severe. Thinness is equated with beauty, success, wealth, style, and the ability to find a boyfriend or a husband. Basically, thin is everything in our culture.

But, girls can lose everything by devoting themselves to being thin. Eating disorders make girls physically weak and ill. Girls can lose interest in activities they used to enjoy. Relationships and friendships may become impossible to maintain when someone is completely focused on what she is eating.

Many times, the very behaviors that lead to an eating disorder make it worse over time. A girl who forces herself not to eat may find that eventually she is physically unable to eat. An outgoing girl may become quiet, tired, and depressed.

Also, many girls use food and diet as a way to deal with other emotions. Whether they eat too much or too little, girls may act out how they are feeling inside by what they put in their mouths. The problem with eating disorders is that many girls get positive attention by using food in this dangerous and misguided way.

Get Healthy

1. Talk to your friends about eating disorders. Make a pact with each other that you will be healthy instead of just skinny.

2. Look for normal-sized girls in music, film, and television as role models. People are finally realizing that other images need to be available for adolescent girls besides the super skinny ones.

3. Don't weigh yourself, and don't count calories. It is okay to eat some fatty or sugary foods. Healthful diets are about balance.

The Last Word from Ashley

It is very scary to think about the risks that go along with eating disorders. But it is also scary to think about so many girls obsessing over their diets instead of enjoying their lives. If girls weren't so worried about being thin, think of all the other fun stuff they could be doing while growing up to be healthy young women.

A Second Look

Now that we've talked about all the messed-up stuff that can happen to your body during adolescence, I hope you feel better. Seriously! You're not the only girl worrying about the way that you look. Actually, you'd be the weird one if you were totally happy with your body all the time. But you don't have to let the body blues rule your life.

Whether you've got a big butt or no butt, you can make a choice to quit obsessing about it. Only then can you get on with the rest of your life—you know, the part that has nothing to do with your butt.

Once you've made the choice to stop trying to be perfect, you might find that you actually like some of your so-called imperfections. They are, after all, part of what makes you special.

Besides, think of how boring the world would be if everyone looked and dressed exactly the same. Loving your unique self—and accepting your unique body—is a big part of loving life!

But even if you never learn to love every single part, hopefully you'll love yourself enough to quit hating and take care of your body. After all, your body is going to be with you for a very long time.

XOXO,
Ashley

Pay It Forward

Remember, a healthful life is about balance. Now that you know how to walk that path, pay it forward to a friend or even to yourself! Remember the Get Healthy tips throughout this book, and read the steps below to get healthy and get going.

- Make a list of things you are good at that have nothing to do with your size or your body. Enjoy what you've got. You can't change what nature gave you, so don't hide it. Try to see the beauty in each individual part of yourself instead of worrying about how it looks to other people. Try to comment on other people's differences in a positive way.

- Don't keep your questions and fears to yourself. Find a trusted adult to talk with and help you find answers to your questions.

- Get together with your friends. Talk to them about eating disorders. Talk to each other about what you're going through with body changes. Make a pact with each other to be healthy and stay positive.

- Get into yoga. It is one sport that encourages health and peacefulness inside you as opposed to weight loss. Don't weigh yourself, and don't count calories. It is okay to eat some fatty or sugary foods.

- Try making a recipe from a healthy cookbook that will taste good and give you energy. Get outside to relax and breathe some fresh air.

- Try volunteering. Talk to a coach, a counselor, or a school nutritionist to see if she will be your group mentor. Once you have organized like-minded friends, volunteer to help somewhere. You could go to a food kitchen, a shelter, or a local library. When you're not as focused on yourself, you can find that helping others in need is a great way to improve your own self-esteem!

- Think of the reasons you respect certain people. Many of those great traits are what's on the inside. Remember, our bodies change throughout our entire lives. Your body should never hold you back—it is a vehicle to help you get the most out of your life!

Additional Resources

Selected Bibliography

Glennon, Will. *200 Ways to Raise a Girl's Self-Esteem: An Indispensable Guide for Parents, Teachers & Other Concerned Caregivers*. Berkeley, CA: Conari Press, 1999.

Hartley-Brewer, Elizabeth. *Raising Confident Girls: 100 Tips for Parents and Teachers*. Cambridge, MA: Fisher Books, 2001.

Pipher, Mary Bray. *Reviving Ophelia: Saving the Selves of Adolescent Girls*. New York, NY: Putnam, 1994.

Further Reading

Brody, Janis. *Your Body: The Girls' Guide*. New York, NY: St. Martin, 2000.

DeVillers, Julia. *GirlWise: How to Be Confident, Capable, Cool, and in Control*. Roseville, CA: Prima Pub., 2002.

Edut, Ophira. Ed. *Body Outlaws: Rewriting the Rules of Beauty and Body Image*. Emeryville, CA: Seal Press, PGW, 2003.

Web Sites

To learn more about physical changes and body image, visit ABDO Publishing Company on the World Wide Web at **www.abdopublishing.com**. Web sites about physical changes and body image are featured on our Book Links page. These links are routinely monitored and updated to provide the most current information available.

For More Information

For more information on this subject, contact or visit the following organizations.

I Am B.E.A.U.T.I.F.U.L.

I AM, INC.
4850 Golden Parkway, Suite B-230, Buford, GA 30518
404-545-9051
www.iambeautiful.org
This organization is designed to empower girls in all areas of their lives. The group features an annual Unsung Heroine Award, as well as national programs, volunteer opportunities, and camps.

girlshealth.gov

Attn.: girlshealth.gov
8270 Willow Oaks Corporate Drive, Suite 301, Fairfax, VA 22031
www.girlshealth.gov/mind/feelinggood.htm
Designed to give healthy, logical advice on health issues, this government program offers a number of tips, ideas, and suggestions for getting through girlhood.

Girls, Inc.

120 Wall Street, New York, NY 10005
800-374-4475
www.girlsinc-online.org/members/Welcome.html
A leader in the girls' rights movement, this leadership group offers online support and information, as well as advocacy movements in Washington DC.

Glossary

accusation
A claim or statement that someone has done something wrong.

anorexia
Also called anorexia nervosa, a medical condition in which a person has an obsessive desire to lose weight by not eating.

bulimia
Also called bulimia nervosa, a medical condition in which a person compulsively overeats, and then purges, or throws up, the food.

disorder
Abnormal physical or mental conditions that require medical treatment.

diverse
Having a great deal of variety.

infertile
Not able to reproduce children.

isolate
To cause someone to be alone or apart from other people.

lesbian
   A homosexual woman.

obsession
   An idea or thought that a person cannot stop focusing on and is continually preoccupied with.

seizure
   A sudden fit or attack of illness resulting in convulsions, which are irregular muscle movements.

vicious
   Intentionally violent or cruel.

violate
   To harm or disrespect someone, especially in a sexual way.

Index

About the Author

Ashley Harris lives and works in Chicago, Illinois, where she completed an MA from the University of Chicago. Her research focused on how Web culture has impacted adolescent girls' body image and sense of identity. Her work has appeared in *VenusZine* and *Time Out Chicago*. She enjoys live music, bike riding, and spending time with the many friends whose experiences helped her write this book.

Photo Credits

Image Source/AP Images, 12; Lauren Greenfield/AP Images, 20; Keith Brofsky/Jupiterimages/AP Images, 30; SW Productions/Jupiterimages/AP Images, 38; Nicole Katano/Jupiterimages/AP Images, 43, 65, 92; Image Source/AP Images, 48; Rob Melnychuk/Jupiterimages/AP Images, 51; Sean Locke/iStockphoto, 56; Lisa F. Young/iStockphoto, 60; Paul Kline/iStockphoto, 74; Lev Olkha/iStockphoto, 77; Kiichiro Sato/AP Images, 87; iStockphoto, 96